W9-DFC-328

Our Amazing States™

Iowa

The Hawkeye State

Marcia Amidon Lusted

PowerKiDS press.
New York

For all my friends in Cedar Rapids, Iowa

Published in 2010 by The Rosen Publishing Group, Inc.
29 East 21st Street, New York, NY 10010

First Edition

Editor: Nicole Pristash
Book Layout: Julio Gil
Book Design: Greg Tucker
Photo Researcher: Jessica Gerweck

Photo Credits: Cover © www.iStockphoto.com/Skip ODonnell; p. 5 © Walter Bibikow/JAI/Corbis; p. 7 MPI/Getty Images; p. 9 Panoramic Images/Getty Images; p. 11 © www.iStockphoto.com/4loops; p. 13 © www.iStockphoto.com/Lynn Graesing; p. 15 © Corbis; p. 17 Scott Olson/Getty Images; p. 19 Courtesy of the National Park Service; p. 22 (tree, rock, flag, bird) Shutterstock.com; p. 22 (flower) © www.iStockphoto.com/Steve Geer; p. 22 (Buffalo Bill) Hulton Archive/Getty Images; p. 22 (Herbert Hoover) Stock Montage/Getty Images; p. 22 (Ashton Kutcher) David Greedy/Getty Images.

Library of Congress Cataloging-in-Publication Data

Lusted, Marcia Amidon.
Iowa : the Hawkeye State / Marcia Amidon Lusted. — 1st ed.
p. cm. — (Our amazing states)
Includes index.
ISBN 978-1-4358-9348-1 (library binding) — ISBN 978-1-4358-9790-8 (pbk.) —
ISBN 978-1-4358-9791-5 (6-pack)
1. Iowa—Juvenile literature. I. Title.
F621.3.L87 2010
977.7—dc22

2009027604

Manufactured in the United States of America

CPSIA Compliance Information: Batch #WW10PK: For Further Information contact Rosen Publishing, New York, New York at 1-800-237-9932

Contents

This Is the Place

There is a state whose name comes from a Native American word that means "this is the place." Here, farmers grow soybeans and tall stalks of corn. Where are we? We are in Iowa! Iowa is found in the upper midwestern part of the United States. Minnesota lies to the north, and Missouri is south.

Iowa's nickname is the Hawkeye State. It honors Chief Black Hawk, a leader of the Sauk Indians who once lived in Iowa. During his time there, he and his people fought against the government in a war called the Black Hawk War. The government had taken the Sauks' land in Illinois, and Black Hawk wanted it back. Black Hawk lost the fight, but he is remembered for his strong will.

Farms, such as the one shown here, are common sights in Iowa. In 2007, there were more than 92,000 farms in the state.

People lived in the area now known as Iowa as far back as 13,000 years ago. These people **roamed** and hunted large animals, such as mastodons. Later groups built burial mounds from dirt and stones in the area.

In 1673, Frenchmen Louis Joliet and Father Jacques Marquette explored the area, and France soon claimed it. In 1803, France sold Iowa to the United States as part of the **Louisiana Purchase**. President Thomas Jefferson then sent two explorers, Meriwether Lewis and William Clark, to search for a path to the Pacific Ocean. Iowa was one of the areas through which they traveled in 1804. Soon, pioneers came to the area, settled, and built farms there. Iowa became the twenty-ninth state in 1846.

This artwork shows Lewis and Clark having a council, or meeting, with Native Americans near Iowa's border. The town of Council Bluffs, Iowa, was named after this meeting.

Plains, Hills, and Rivers

Glaciers that covered the area thousands of years ago shaped much of the landscape in Iowa. Because of these glaciers, some parts of Iowa are flat plains while other areas have gentle rolling hills and valleys. Many of Iowa's lakes were formed when the glaciers left large holes, which later filled with water. Iowa is the only state that has rivers large enough for shipping on its western edge and eastern edge. The Missouri River is to the west and the Mississippi River is to the east.

Iowa winters can get very cold. The coldest **temperature** ever recorded in Iowa was -47° F (-44° C)! Iowa summers are very hot and humid, and the state is known for having as many as 30 **tornadoes** each year.

Here you can see the tall limestone cliffs that are found along the upper Iowa River.

Full of Game

A visitor to Iowa in 1833 said that he had never seen a place so full of **game**. Some of the animals he may have seen include white-tailed deer, rabbits, and chickens. Many other animals are found in Iowa. Bald eagles nest near rivers. Bears and bobcats are sometimes seen, too.

Trees, such as silver maples and cottonwoods, grow near rivers in Iowa. Oak and hickory trees are found in higher areas. Many different types of prairie flowers, like the purple aster, are found on the plains. There are tall prairie grasses, too. At one time, these grasses grew as tall as 6 feet (2 m)! Iowa's state flower is the pink wild prairie rose. You can see it in summer.

In Iowa, rabbits can be found in meadows and forests. They eat grass, leaves, and plants.

What's Made in Iowa?

Although Iowa is known for its farms, manufacturing is a big part of the state's **economy**. At the Quaker Oats factory, corn and oats grown in Iowa are used to make breakfast cereals. Corn syrup and other foods are also made in the state. A company called Pioneer Hi-Bred creates new kinds of seeds that are easier for farmers to grow. The biggest popcorn-packing plant in the United States is in Iowa.

Other factories make farming **equipment**, such as tractors and harvesters. Many popular magazines, such as *Better Homes and Gardens*, are created there as well. Iowa mines produce sand, **gravel**, and gypsum, a **mineral** that is used to make **cement**.

Many ethanol fuel plants, like this one, are found in Iowa. Ethanol fuel is often made from grain and corn.

Farm Country

Iowa has some of the richest soil in the country. The state is sometimes called America's breadbasket because so many of the grains we eat are grown there. Iowa is the nation's biggest producer of corn. Soybeans and oats are grown there, too.

In the northeastern part of Iowa, where the land is hilly and not as good for growing crops, there are many dairy farms. Supplying cattle for beef and hogs for pork to the rest of the country, Iowa is one of the biggest producers of livestock in America. There are around 92,000 farms in Iowa. Because it is expensive to buy farm equipment and land, though, big companies now own many of these farms instead of families.

Soybean farms, such as this one, are plentiful in Iowa. In 2007, there were more than 8 million acres (3 million ha) of soybean fields in the state.

Wonderful Des Moines

Iowa's capital city is Des Moines, and it is found near the center of the state. Des Moines is the most populated city in the state. More than 190,000 people live there.

In Des Moines, you can visit the Botanical Center where there are flowers even in the middle of winter. You can ride the nearby Boone & Scenic Valley Railroad or learn what it was like to live on a farm in the pioneer days at Living History Farms. More than a million visitors come to Des Moines every August for the Iowa State Fair, where you can taste foods grown in Iowa, listen to music, and ride a roller coaster. You can even see a cow sculpted, or shaped, out of 600 pounds (272 kg) of butter!

This woman is waiting to show her cow at the Iowa State Fair. At a cattle competition, or contest, a judge picks which cow he would be most likely to buy.

Mounds of Earth

Another popular place to visit in Iowa is **Effigy** Mounds National Monument, near Harpers Ferry. Over 2,000 years ago, a group of Native Americans called the Woodland people lived in the area. Over time, these people built more than 200 mounds made out of dirt and rocks. Around 30 of these mounds are shaped like birds and bears. These mounds are effigies. The mounds were built to honor the people's dead loved ones and their beliefs.

Today, visitors to Effigy Mounds National Monument can see many of these mounds in person. Visitors can walk on the trails around the area and learn more about the people who created these interesting mounds.

This picture shows part of the Marching Bear Group at Effigy Mounds National Monument. This group of mounds has 10 bears, 3 birds, and 2 line-shaped mounds.

Come to the Heartland

Iowa is often called America's Heartland. Like America itself, Iowa has both cities and small towns. It has as busy streets and quiet, less-traveled roads. Iowa is full of fun things to do. You can visit the famous cornfield from the movie *Field of Dreams* in Dyersville. You can visit an **Amish** market in Kalona, where horses and **buggies** are tied up outside. You can also take a steamboat ride on the Mississippi River.

Whether it is growing corn and soybeans that feed a hungry country or making computers and other products, Iowa is an important state. It is no wonder that so many people make Iowa their home!

Glossary

Amish (AH-mish) A group of people who believe in living simply.

buggies (BUH-geez) Small, light vehicles pulled by horses.

cement (sih-MENT) A mix of water, sand, and rock that hardens. It is often used for building.

economy (ih-KAH-nuh-mee) The way in which a country or a business oversees its goods and services.

effigy (EH-fuh-jee) A figure that represents a real person or animal.

equipment (uh-KWIP-mint) All the supplies needed to do something.

game (GAYM) Wild animals that are hunted for food.

gravel (GRA-vel) Small, loose stones used to line paths and roads.

Louisiana Purchase (loo-ee-zee-AN-uh PUR-chus) Land that the United States bought from France in 1803.

mineral (MIN-rul) A natural element that is not a living thing.

roamed (ROHMD) Walked around with no special plan.

temperature (TEM-pur-cher) How hot or cold something is.

tornadoes (taw-NAY-dohz) Funnel-shaped clouds that produce strong, spinning winds.

Iowa State Symbols

State Tree
Oak

State Rock
Geode

State Flag

State Bird
Eastern Goldfinch

State Flower
Wild Prairie Rose

State Seal

Famous People from Iowa

William F. "Buffalo Bill" Cody
(1846 – 1917)
Born in Le Claire, IA
Wild West Showman

Herbert Hoover
(1874–1964)
Born in West Branch, IA
U.S. President

Ashton Kutcher
(1978–)
Born in Cedar Rapids, IA
Actor

Iowa State Map

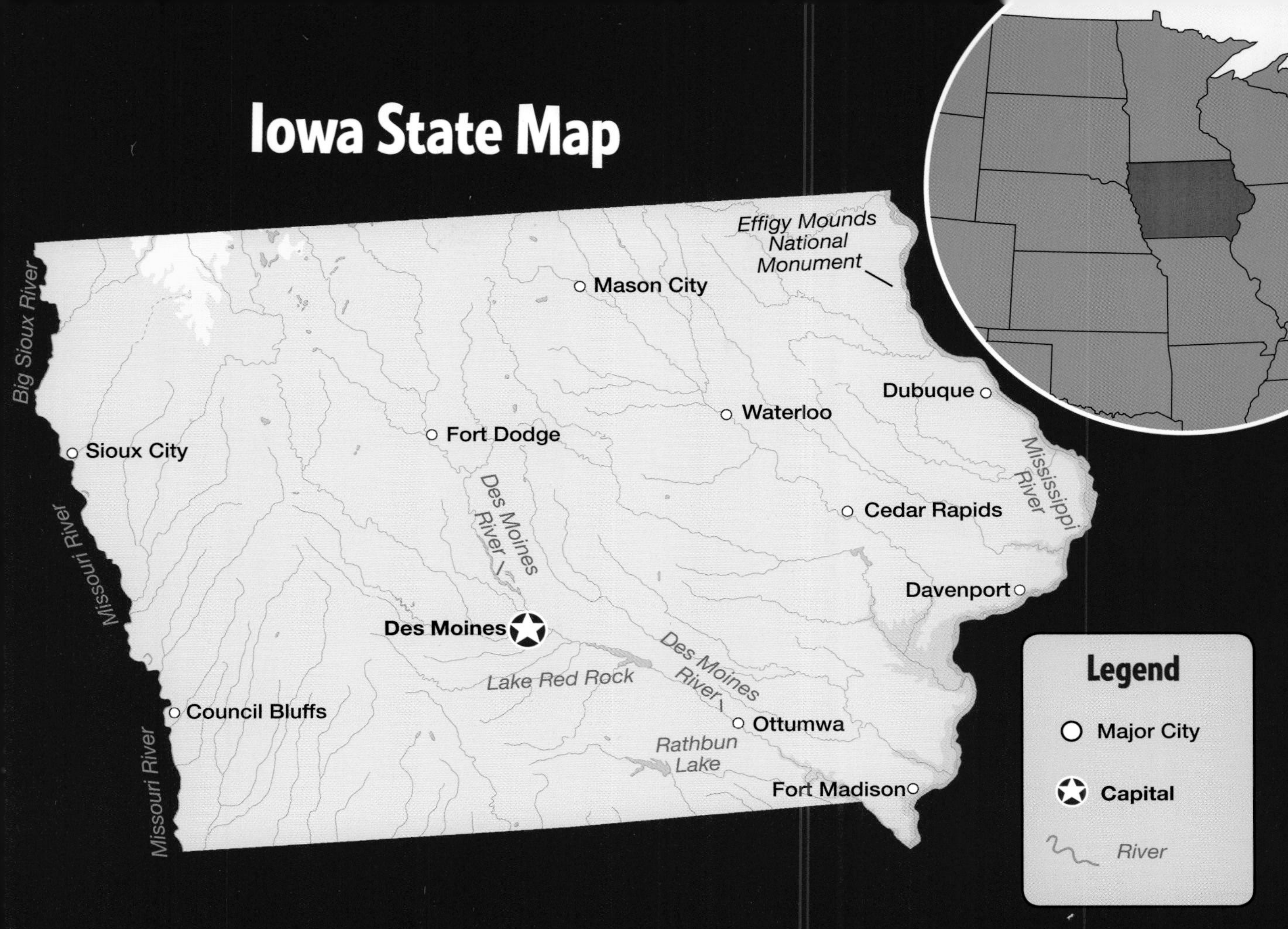

Iowa State Facts

Population: About 2,926,381

Area: 56,275 square miles (145,752 sq km)

Motto: "Our liberties we prize and our rights we will maintain"

Song: "The Song of Iowa," words by S. H. M. Byers

Index

Web Sites

Due to the changing nature of Internet links, PowerKids Press has developed an online list of Web sites related to the subject of this book. This site is updated regularly. Please use this link to access the list:
www.powerkidslinks.com/amst/ia/